PRAYER PRAISE & PROMISES

A DAILY WALK THROUGH THE PSALMS

by Warren W. Wiersbe

BAKER BOOK HOUSE
Grand Rapids, Michigan 49516

29,000 printed to date—1995
(1155-054—3.5M—55)
ISBN 0-8010-9725-8

Unless otherwise noted, all Scripture quotations are from
The New King James Version.

Printed in the United States of America.

FOREWORD

The Psalms have always held a special place in the affection of Israel. The people of God rejoiced and lamented together by singing the Psalms. The early Christians discovered the Psalms to be an integral link to their heritage as well.

A psalm was the expression of joy uttered by Augustine at his conversion, and a psalm was the consolation on his lips as he lay upon his death bed. Chrysostom comforted himself in exile by quoting the Psalms. John Hus had a psalm on his lips as he was burned at the stake. Reciting a psalm, Luther entered the Diet of Worms, prepared to defy the Church and stand by faith alone.

But the Psalms have meant much more to us than affection or motivation. They also have been a significant source of inspiration. A. C. Gabelein used to say, "A psalm a day keeps worry away." Many of us have found the Psalms to be an excellent source of comfort, of courage, of strength.

Strength and hope for our spiritual journey is the goal of Warren Wiersbe in this daily devotional on the Psalms, and he succeeds very well. Writing in his own practical and interesting style, Dr. Wiersbe brings us to the banquet table and serves a heaping portion of God's blessing and strength through each psalm. Every reader will be blessed, but more than that, every reader will be instructed, motivated, inspired and challenged.

Here you will find daily food in abundance—good food, tasty food, food to fuel your Christian life. If a psalm a day does keep worry away, who of us can afford to be without one? This devotional book will ensure that your minimum daily Psalms requirement is met. Bon appetit!

Woodrow Kroll

PREFACE TO GOD'S HYMNAL

Have you ever read the preface to the hymnal used in your church? Few people ever do. The preface to God's hymnal (the Book of Psalms) is Psalm 1. It begins with a word we often use—*blessed*. Nowhere does Scripture tell us that God blesses programs or promotions. But it does teach that He blesses individuals. He blessed Abraham so he might be a blessing to others. And He blesses us so we might bless others.

What you delight in is what will direct your life, so be careful what you enjoy. The blessed person delights in the Law of the Lord (v. 2). He delights so much in the Word of God that he *meditates* on it during the day. Meditation is to the soul what digestion is to the body. It means assimilating the Word of God.

The blessed person is like a tree (v. 3). A tree has roots. The most important part of your life is your "root system." Don't be like the ungodly, who are like chaff (v. 4). Chaff doesn't have roots. It is blown away by every wind that comes along. Your root system is important because it determines your nourishment. It also determines your stability and your strength when the storm comes and the wind starts to blow.

People can't see your root system, but God can. Praying and meditating on the Word of God will cause your roots to go down deep into His love.

♦   ♦   ♦

God delights in blessing His children. But we must prepare ourselves for His blessings by first appropriating the resources He has given us. Delight in the Word of God and feed on it. But do more than occasionally read the Word; meditate on it constantly. Make it your source of spiritual nourishment, and God will bless you with strength and stability.

Separated and Saturated

Two of the most popular words in the Christian vocabulary are *bless* and *blessing*. God wants to bless His people. He wants them to be recipients and channels of blessing. God blesses us to make us a blessing to others, but He has given us certain conditions for receiving blessings.

First, *we must be separated from the world* (v. 1). The world is anything that separates us from God or causes us to disobey Him. Separation is not isolation but contact without contamination. Sin is usually a gradual process. Notice the gradual decline of the sinner in verse 1. He is *walking* (Mark 14:54), *standing* (John 18:18) and then *sitting* (Luke 22:55). Becoming worldly is progressive; it happens by degrees. We make friends with the world; we become spotted by the world; we love the world, become confirmed to it and end up condemned with it. Lot is an example of someone who became worldly. He looked toward Sodom, pitched his tent toward Sodom, lived there, lost everything and ended in sin.

Second, *we must be saturated with the Word* (v. 2). Whatever delights us directs us. We saturate ourselves with the Word by meditating on it. Meditation is to the spirit what digestion is to the body. When we meditate on the Word, we allow the Spirit of God within us to "digest" the Word of God for us. So not only do we delight in the Word, it becomes a source of spiritual nourishment for us.

Enjoy the blessings God has for you and allow Him to make you a blessing to others. (A third condition, being situated by the waters, is the topic of our next devotional.)

♦ ♦ ♦

God desires to bless us, but we must meet His conditions for receiving blessings. By staying separate from the world and keeping saturated in the Word, we may expect God's blessings. Resolve to meditate on the Word of God and obey it. He will make you a blessing to others.

Are You Situated by the Waters?

A tree is a blessing. It holds soil, provides shade and produces fruit. The godly are like trees, with root systems that go deep into the spiritual resources of God's grace (v. 3). But sadly, many professing Christians are not like trees but are like artificial plants or cut flowers with no roots. They may be beautiful for a while, but soon they die.

A tree needs light, water and roots to live. We all have resources upon which we draw life. The question we need to ask ourselves is, Where are our roots? The person God can bless is planted by the rivers of water. We must be careful not to be like Christians who are dry and withered and depend upon their own resources. They are like tumbleweeds, blown about by any wind of doctrine.

To have the blessings of verse 3, we need to meet the conditions of verses 1 and 2. That is, we must first be separated from the world and saturated with the Word to be situated by the waters.

God desires to bless us, but we need to meet certain conditions to receive His blessings. We bear fruit only when we have roots, and we must draw upon spiritual resources to bring forth fruit in due season. To bear the fruit of the Spirit, we must allow the Spirit to work in us and through us.

In contrast to the believer, the ungodly are not like trees but are like chaff. They have no roots, produce no fruit and are blown about. The ungodly reject the Word of God and will perish without hope (v. 6). As Christians we must not reject the ungodly but try to reach them. God blesses us so that we might be a blessing to others. His Spirit helps us bear fruit that can help win the lost.

Are you like a tree or like chaff?

♦   ♦   ♦

We need God's resources to bear fruit. But where we place our roots is paramount. Only as we grow them deeply into the spiritual resources of God's grace will we produce fruit. Make the Bible your spiritual resource. Delight in it and feed your soul with its truth. God can use you to help win the lost.

WHEN GOD LAUGHS

Are you surprised that God laughs? "He who sits in the heavens shall laugh; the Lord shall hold them in derision" (v. 4). God has a sense of humor, but His laughter is the kind that is born of judgment. It's the laughter of derision, the laughter of irony. What is God laughing at? He's laughing at puny little kings and rulers who have united to shake their fists at His throne and tell Him they don't want Him to rule over them (vv. 2,3). God laughs at them because He knows man cannot survive without submitting to His authority. Man is made in the image of God, and if he fights against Him, he fights against himself. Man, in his rebellion, tries to make God in his own image. He thinks God can be treated with disdain and disobedience. And God laughs.

We can laugh when we read the headlines or watch TV reports. We see a world in turmoil, a world united against God, but we laugh because He is still on the throne. "Yet I have set My King on My holy hill of Zion" (v. 6). Jesus Christ is God's King, and He is on the throne. Therefore, we can look at the nations as they are in turmoil, as they unite against God, and we can smile—in fact, we can laugh. They are fighting a losing battle. Jesus Christ is on the throne of the universe, and we who are Christians are seated with Him on that throne.

◆　　◆　　◆

As believers, we are to be witnesses for Christ. Reaching a world that rebels against God's authority can be difficult. Be encouraged, for your efforts will not be wasted. God is in control and one day will bring all governments and earthly powers into submission. Pray that He will use your life to reach others and glorify Himself.

FOUR VOICES
PART 1

The world is getting noisier. So many voices vie for our attention. The result is that many people are getting the wrong instructions. It is important that we have discernment in a noisy world filled with propaganda. We need the truth.

We need to distinguish the four voices of Psalm 2. The first is *the voice of defiance*—the nations of the world (vv. 1-3). It is amazing that the nations would defy Almighty God. He has provided for them (Acts 14:17), guided them (I Tim. 6:17) and determined their histories (Acts 17:26). Why do the nations rebel? They seek freedom without God. P. T. Forsythe said, "The purpose of life is not to find your freedom. The purpose of life is to find your Master." Authority demands submission (Matt. 11:29).

The world is a mess morally, intellectually, socially, politically, economically and ecologically because it has defied God. Man is made in God's image. The irony is that when man rebels against God, he rebels against himself.

Second, we have the *voice of derision*—the voice of God the Father (vv. 4-6). While there is tumult on earth, there is tranquility in heaven. God laughs because the Kingdom is secure; the King has been established. Jesus is God's King. Though the nations rebel, we don't need to worry, for the King is already enthroned in heaven.

Listen to the voice of God. He is laughing at the world's rebellion, and you can laugh with Him if Jesus is your King.

✦   ✦   ✦

The world often tries to drown out the truth. Its voice of defiance is clear. The world's corruption is a result of its defiance. Take inventory of the voices you listen to. Are you part of the voice of defiance, or can you laugh with God at the world's rebellion?

FOUR VOICES
PART 2

A third voice we hear in the world is the *voice of declaration*—God the Son (vv. 7-9). He runs the universe by decree, not by democracy. He knows everything, is everywhere and can do anything. God's decrees will succeed. Puny, foolish men with their godless living will not eradicate or hinder His decrees.

God decrees that Jesus Christ is His Son. Jesus is God, and He is King by nature, by conquest and by His Resurrection. He is reigning today, and we can reign in life through Him (Rom. 5:17).

God also decrees that He will break the rebellious nations with "a rod of iron." When His scepter of righteousness goes forth in judgment, the nations will cry out, not in repentance but in rebellion. God already has given the nations to His Son (Matt. 4:8-10).

The fourth voice is the *voice of decision*—the Holy Spirit (vv. 10-12). He wants us to learn—to be wise, to be instructed. Many depend on philosophy, psychology and history. These disciplines are helpful, but Christians must rely first and foremost on the Spirit of God to reveal truth.

The Holy Spirit wants us to be *willing to serve*. We serve the Lord, not sin. There is joy with our fear because God is our Father. In searching for liberty, the rebellious crowd practices anarchy, for freedom without authority is anarchy. We are made in the image of God. To rebel against Him is to rebel against our own nature.

The Holy Spirit also wants us to *be reconciled*. God is reconciled to us through Christ (Acts 16:31). Jesus "kissed" us in His birth and death. Today He is the Lamb, but someday He will come as the Lion to judge. God is holy and will not allow sin and rebellion to go on forever.

♦　　♦　　♦

Are you listening to the right voices? "Blessed are all those who put their trust in Him." We are saved by faith through the death of the Son of God. Are you saved? If not, hear His voice and trust in Him.

ARE YOU
SLEEPING WELL?

How well we sleep sometimes indicates how much we really trust the Lord. David said, "I lay down and slept; I awoke, for the Lord sustained me" (v. 5). We may think we can do that anytime. But what if we had been where David was? He was fleeing from his son Absalom, who had turned against him and had driven him from Jerusalem. Now David was in the wilderness with his army. It would be difficult to lie down and sleep knowing that you are in a dangerous wilderness and that your own son is against you. Oh, it wasn't the physical danger that kept David awake. He knew God would protect him. It was the inner spiritual and emotional agony of having his own flesh and blood trying to seize the kingdom from him.

But David said, in effect, "Lord, You are able to give me peace in my heart, the protection I need, the perspective I need. You are able to help me in the midst of this difficult situation." The heart of every problem is really the problem in the heart. David knew that it was not *the army on the outside* that would keep him awake but *the agony on the inside*.

This psalm starts with David's cry, "Many are they who rise up against me" (v. 1). He's pleading for help. The psalm ends with David's singing a song of praise (v. 8). Your day might begin by your pleading for help. But if you are trusting the Lord, it could end by your praising Him for the help He has given you.

◆   ◆   ◆

Difficult circumstances often rob us of our peace and our perspective. When you find yourself in adverse circumstances or in the face of frightening consequences, admit your trouble and affirm your trust in Him. Then be encouraged that God protects you and gives you peace in the midst of the storm.

BIGGER AND BETTER

Sometimes God's people can be so discouraging! In Psalm 4 we find David listening to people saying, "Who will show us any good?" (v. 6). David's own men were discouraged. They were going through a trial, and some were saying, "O David, this is the end. God is no longer going to help us." That's hard to take. It's rough when your associates or friends say to you, "Well, you've reached the end. Who will show us any good?"

But David called on the Lord, and God enlarged him. "You have relieved [enlarged] me when I was in distress" (v. 1). Pressure on the *outside* should make us bigger on the *inside*. The trials of life will press against us and make us either midgets or giants—either smaller or bigger. But we have to start on the inside. "You have relieved me when I was in distress." How did this happen?

David cried out to God, "You have put gladness in my heart" (v. 7). He started out with sadness and ended with gladness. He started with tears and ended with triumph. Once again he's sleeping beautifully. "I will both lie down in peace, and sleep; for You alone, O Lord, make me dwell in safety" (v. 8).

David discovered that what was important was not the *circumstance around him but the attitude within him.* Let God enlarge you when you are going through distress. He can do it. You can't do it, and others can't do it for you. In fact, others may want to make things even tighter and narrower for you. But when you turn to the Lord and trust Him, He will enlarge you on the inside. You'll come out of your distresses a bigger person because you've trusted in the Lord.

♦   ♦   ♦

There is a relationship between our attitude inside and our circumstances outside. If we maintain the proper attitude, God will use our trials to enlarge us. Are you going through a trial today? Give your circumstances to the Lord and trust Him to enlarge you.

REST IN THE MIDST OF TRIALS

David was experiencing great difficulty. He was in a "tight corner." God permits tight corners (II Sam. 12:10). He forgives but disciplines, and we reap what we sow (Ps. 25:17).

Psalm 4 is encouraging because it tells us that God cares for us and gives us several blessings in the midst of our trials. First, He gives us the *blessing of enlargement* (v. 1). *Relieved* means "enlarged." When God permits enlarged troubles, He enlarges His people; that is, we grow. Joseph is a good example of this (Ps. 18:19,36). His difficulties revealed his character, and he grew. Enlarged troubles lead to an enlarged life, which leads to an enlarged place and enlarged paths. God had an enlarged ministry for David, but He first had to make him grow.

Second, God gives us the *blessing of encouragement* (vv. 2,3). Eventually, all earthly causes will fail. Only the plan of God will succeed. The Lord is our shield, our glory and the One who lifts our head. In this life we will have problems, but God encourages us.

Third, God gives us the *blessing of enablement* (vv. 4,5). Tight corners bring us face to face with trusting versus temptation (Matt. 4:3,4). David had a right to be angry. Anger can be used of God to bring about righteousness, or it can be used by Satan to bring about sin (James 1:20). *Meditate* means "to discuss with yourself." It's so easy to brood when we're lying in bed, but God gives quietness when we meditate (Ps. 46:10).

Fourth, God gives us the *blessings of enlightenment and enjoyment* (vv. 6-8). David's people were discouraged. Are you a discourager or an encourager? As Christians, we should have the smile of God upon us (Num. 6:25). We should exhibit gladness and joy in the Lord. God adds to this the blessing of peace and sleep. This is possible when Christ is Savior. So get your eyes off the enemy and on the Lord. The temptation to sin is great during difficulties, but trust in the Lord, and He will give you peace and joy in the midst of difficulty.

◆　　◆　　◆

God's blessings are designed to do more than simply comfort us in our difficulties; they are to help us grow. Take strength from knowing that God is weaving His purposes into your life and that He will reward your trust in Him. "And we know that God causes all things to work together for good to those who love God, to those who are called according to His purpose" (Rom. 8:28).

A Heart Problem

I t's imperative for us to meet God in the morning if we want to have a good day. Jesus got up early in the morning to pray, according to Mark 1:35. Here we find the psalmist saying, "My voice You shall hear in the morning, O Lord; in the morning I will direct it to You, and I will look up" (v. 3).

When I used to work the night shift, I would sleep in the morning. So when I got up in the afternoon, I would meet with the Lord. Meeting with God is not an appointment on a clock but an appointment in your heart. Does God hear your voice in the morning? When He looks on you at the beginning of your day, does He look on you as a priest who has come to offer Him sacrifices of praise? That's what direct means (v. 3)—"to order my prayer." It means to arrange the sacrifice on the altar.

When you wake up in the morning, remind yourself that you are one of God's priests. How did you become a priest? Through faith in Jesus Christ. "To Him who loved us and washed us from our sins in His own blood, and has made us kings and priests to His God and Father" (Rev. 1:5,6). You're one of God's priests. That means wherever you are is God's temple, because your body is His temple.

The first thing we do in the morning is the first thing the high priest used to do every morning. He laid the burnt offering on the altar. The burnt offering is a picture of total dedication to God. If you want to have a good day, start by giving yourself to the Lord as a burnt offering, a living sacrifice, holy and acceptable to God (Rom. 12:1). A good day begins in the morning, and it begins at the altar.

♦   ♦   ♦

Does your day begin with God? If not, decide to start each morning by dedicating yourself to Him as a living sacrifice and ask His guidance for the day's decisions and actions. He wants to direct your life. So view each day as a gift from God and determine to be a good steward of the day's resources. Make your time with Him a daily appointment.

REQUEST, REASON AND RESPONSE IN THE MIDST OF TRIALS

What do you do in difficult situations? Many of the psalms were written during difficult, often painful, experiences. In Psalm 5 we find two sequences concerning trials. In the first sequence (vv. 1-7), David is experiencing difficulty and makes his request—"hear me." (v. 1-3). *Meditation* here means "sighing, murmuring, groaning"—a quiet expression of feelings. When our burden is beyond expression, all we can do is sigh and moan before the Lord. The Spirit hears our groanings and intercedes for us (Rom. 8:26). David's meditation turns to a cry (v. 2; Heb. 5:7). Prayer is not always a quiet, joyful conversation with God. Sometimes it is a battle against the principalities arrayed against us.

David's reason for making this request is the holiness of God (vv. 4-6). He cried to God because He is holy and stands against the wicked and boastful. Although He will judge the wicked, God does not always judge sin immediately. David's response is worship (v. 7), individual and personal.

In the second sequence, David makes another request—"lead me" (v. 8). He wants God's way, which is the righteous way. In the midst of difficulty, what we need most is wisdom to know the will of God (James 1:5). Notice that David asks to be led, not delivered. God has a straight way through every difficulty that will lead us to victory.

His reason this time is the wickedness of man (vv. 9,10). Destruction means "a yawning, open abyss." An open tomb pictures defilement and death. Flattery is not communication; it is manipulation. Absalom fell by his own counsel. David did nothing. He let God do it all (Rom. 12:19).

David's response (vv. 11,12) is rejoicing in faith, love and hope. Joy comes from trusting in and loving the Lord. This kind of joy comes from God's work on the inside, not from circumstances on the outside.

The psalmist tells us to expect difficulty. We shouldn't run from our trials but bring to God our requests, our reasons and our response.

♦   ♦   ♦

You need never be paralyzed by your difficulties. You have the privilege of praying to a loving, understanding Father, who knows your condition. He guides you through difficulty to victory. When your faith, hope and love are fixed on the Lord, you can face any difficulty or problem, and God will give you joy and peace within.

WORSE
THAN DEATH

All of us know what it means to sin and to confess our sin. Psalm 6 is the first of the seven penitential psalms. Occasionally God has to remind us to confess our sins.

In verses 1-5 David pleads for God not to rebuke him or to chasten him. God's chastening is not punishment. It builds our Christian character. Hebrews 12 talks about chastening, and the word used means "child training." It's the picture of a child learning how to be a good athlete. God chastens us, but He does so in love. David was afraid that God was going to chasten him in His hot displeasure (v. 1). But our God is a God of mercy and grace. This doesn't mean, however, that we can minimize sin. This doesn't mean we should ever say, "Well, God is a forgiving God; therefore, I can do whatever I want to do, and He will forgive me." No, David was saying, "Lord, I've sinned. I'm weary with my groaning. Forgive me. I have done wrong." And God does forgive those who confess their sins to Him.

Sin is the Christian's worst possible experience. It's far worse than pain or suffering or even death itself. We are weak, and sometimes we fail. But let's never be afraid to come to our Father with our appeal for forgiveness. The tragedy is that all around us, enemies are waiting for us to fall. They want to point at us and say, "See, that Christian failed." But we can come before the Lord and ask Him for His forgiveness, and He will grant it to us. God will have mercy on us. "Whoever calls on the name of the Lord shall be saved" (Acts 2:21).

◆　　　◆　　　◆

We must never treat sin lightly. Certainly, no Christian should ever harbor sin. But when we do sin, we may lean on God's mercy and grace and confess our sin to a loving Father. One of the great encouragements of the Christian life is that God forgives and restores. Are you living with unconfessed sin? Avoid God's chastening. Confess your sin and ask for His forgiveness.

TESTED IN A TIGHT SPOT

This psalm was born out of a sad experience David had with Cush, a Benjamite (see I Sam. 24-26). Cush was one of Saul's spies. And because of what David did, Cush caused the deaths of innocent men.

Whenever David had a problem with persecution or with people, he would run to God. "O Lord my God, in You I put my trust; save me from all those who persecute me; and deliver me" (v. 1). David's enemies were pursuing him. But the first thing he did was examine his own heart. "O Lord my God, if I have done this: if there is iniquity in my hands" (v. 3). He was saying, "If I have sinned, then let the enemy persecute me."

When we are persecuted or experiencing problems, the first thing we should do is examine our own hearts—not examine the enemy or even examine God by saying, "God, why did You allow such a thing to happen?" When you find yourself in a tight spot, look in the mirror and say, "Father, is there something in my life You are talking to me about? Is there some area in my life where I am not as yielded as I ought to be?"

You may ask, "What about my enemies? Who's going to take care of them?" That was David's question. The answer is that God will take care of the enemy. The wickedness of others will come to an end. Our righteous God will accomplish His purposes, but notice the end of verse 9: "For the righteous God tests the hearts and minds." Times of trial are not only times of testimony and trusting; they are also times of testing. When God tests you, He is showing you your own heart. You may say, "I know my own heart." But you don't. "The heart is deceitful above all things, and desperately wicked; who can know it?" (Jer. 17:9).

♦   ♦   ♦

God has a purpose for trials and testings. Do you find yourself in a tight spot today? Don't view this as something to endure. Rather, consider it an opportunity for growth. Use this time to examine your heart. Perhaps God wants to teach you something and develop an area of your life. Yield yourself to Him and trust Him to do a good work in you.

GIVING BIRTH TO A MONSTER

This passage presents a frightening picture. We read about swords and arrows, pits, ditches and death. God is angry and is judging sin, and He hears David's petition about his persecutors: "O Lord, they are accusing me of something I didn't do. They are lying about me." That's tough to take. People lied about the Lord Jesus, too. And anyone who tries to live like Him is going to suffer this kind of persecution. David's enemies wanted to kill him. Some innocent men had been killed because of him. But David was praying that God would first cleanse his own heart. He said, "Examine me. Look at me. Test me. I want to be sure my life is ruled by integrity."

Sin brings its own judgment. "Behold, the wicked travails with iniquity, conceives trouble and brings forth falsehood" (v. 14). This is a picture of pregnancy and birth. When a person conceives sin and then gives birth to it, he gives birth to a monster that will turn on him and destroy him. David changed the picture in verses 15 and 16: "He made a pit and dug it out, and has fallen into the ditch which he made. His trouble shall return upon his own head." That's a word of encouragement and also a warning. We can't give birth to sin without having to live with the baby, watching it grow up and create problems. Yes, God in His grace forgives. But God in His government says, "We must reap what we sow."

The warning here is don't give birth to sin. There's also an encouragement: If others are giving birth to sin, don't fret over it but pray for them.

✦   ✦   ✦

What is your response when others do their worst to you? Be encouraged that God knows what is happening and will judge sin. If you take care of yourself and walk with integrity, you may be confident that God will deal with those who sin against you. Above all, don't give birth to sin yourself; rather, pray for those who persecute you. God will one day turn your persecution into praise.

LIVE LIKE A KING

Psalm 8 deals with sovereignty. "O Lord, our Lord, how excellent is Your name in all the earth, You who set Your glory above the heavens!" (v. 1). The first Lord means "Jehovah," the covenant-keeping God, the God who keeps His promises. The second Lord means "the Sovereign," the One who has not only the ability but the authority. "O Lord [the promise-making God], our Lord [the Sovereign, who has the power to keep His promises], how excellent is your name in all the earth."

When God saved you, He made you a king. You may not look like one or act like one, but you are one. Your day of salvation was a day of coronation. God put you on the throne through Jesus Christ. Then why do you live like a slave?

We discover in this psalm that God gave Adam and Eve the first crowns. But what did they do? They handed their crowns and scepters to Satan, because they wanted to become like God, to be sovereign. And they lost their dominion. Man today does not have dominion over beasts and fowl and fish. But Jesus does. He had dominion over the fowl: He told a rooster to crow when Peter sinned. He had dominion over the fish: He gathered them into the net when Peter was fishing. He even had dominion over the animals of the field: He rode on a donkey that no one had ever ridden before.

We've lost that dominion, but we've regained our spiritual dominion in Jesus Christ. You were saved to live like a king. Don't live like a slave.

♦   ♦   ♦

Believers have a responsibility to live like kings. Our kingship securely rests on the authority and character of God. Are you living beneath your station? Determine to live like a king.

WHAT IS MAN?

What is man? Charles Darwin said man is an animal. Sigmund Freud taught that man is a spoiled child. Karl Marx believed man is an economic factor. But the Bible says God has a much higher calling for man. God wants us to be kings; He wants us to reign in life. In Psalm 8 we see three different kings exemplified in Adam, Jesus and David.

First, God the Father created us to be kings (Gen. 1:26-28). God gave Adam dominion over the earth. We are created in the image of God with a mind, heart, will and spirit. But sin has marred God's image in man. His mind can't think God's thoughts; his emotions are wrapped up in sin; his will is rebellious, and his spirit is dead.

Second, God the Son redeemed us to be kings. The tragedy of man's rejecting Christ as Savior is that he goes through life as a slave, not a sovereign. Because of his rebellion, man lost his dominion. But Christ's death, Resurrection and Ascension regained what Adam lost—and much more (Rom. 5). Our Lord is reigning today, and we will someday reign with Him.

Third, God the Holy Spirit anointed us to live as kings. Our kingship comes from God. The power of His Spirit gave David the strength to kill Goliath. We are either a sovereign or a slave; either we will reign as kings, or sin will reign in our lives.

God never intended that we live like slaves but that we live like kings and reign over our circumstances and feelings. Trust Christ as Savior to reign in your life.

◆　◆　◆

Do you find yourself a slave to a particular circumstance or emotion? Because of the sacrifice of Christ, we need no longer live as slaves in this world. Claim the power of God's Spirit and live as a king.

YOUR SONG OF VICTORY

P salm 9 is a great victory psalm. "I will praise You, O Lord, with my whole heart; I will tell of all Your marvelous works" (v. 1). Notice the universals in that verse—"my whole heart" and "all Your marvelous works." I must confess that there are times when I don't praise the Lord with my whole heart. At times I've stood in church with the hymnbook in my hand, singing a great song of praise—but not with my whole heart. The best way to have victory is to praise the Lord wholeheartedly.

Granted, there are times when it's hard to praise Him. Think of Paul and Silas in prison (Acts 16:16-34). They had been humiliated. Their rights had been stripped away from them. Their bodies were hurting. Yet they were wholeheartedly praising the Lord. God can heal your broken heart if you give Him all the pieces. He'll put it back together again and give you wholehearted praise.

Don't praise God only about circumstances; praise Him for who He is. "I will be glad and rejoice in You" (v. 2). Maybe you can't rejoice in your circumstances or in the way you feel. Maybe you can't even rejoice in the plans that are made for today, but you always can rejoice in the Lord (Phil. 4:4). You can rejoice in the Lord today because He is worthy of your praise. "I will be glad and rejoice in You; I will sing praise to Your name, O Most High" (v. 2).

The thrust of this psalm is simply this: If your cause is right, God is on your side. He is on His throne, and He is administering His world the way He wants to. David didn't quite understand all that God was doing, but he knew that God knew what He was doing. So when your cause is right, you can praise the Lord, even in the midst of apparent defeat. When God is on the throne, everything turns out all right.

◆   ◆   ◆

If your life is broken right now, be encouraged that God knows what is going on in your life and will restore you. Until He does, rejoice in Him and praise His name.

SAFEST PROTECTION IN THE WORLD

This passage teaches a great truth: The safest and strongest protection we have is the name of the Lord. "And those who know Your name will put their trust in You; for You, Lord, have not forsaken those who seek You" (v. 10). As I read those words, I'm reminded that God forsook His Son for us. Jesus said from the cross, "My God, My God, why have You forsaken Me?" (Matt. 27:46). Has it ever occurred to you that the only person God ever really forsook was His own Son? "He who did not spare His own Son, but delivered Him up for us all" (Rom. 8:32). Because He did this, we can be sure He will never forsake us for the sake of His Son. The Father loves His Son and says to Him, "You have died for these people. I will never forsake them." God's promise to us is "I will never leave you nor forsake you" (Heb. 13:5). "Lo, I am with you always" was our Lord's last statement in the Gospel of Matthew (28:20).

The safest place in all the world is in the will of God, and the safest protection in all the world is the name of God. When you know His name, you know His nature. His names and titles reveal His nature. They tell us who He is and what He can do. For example, He is Jehovah, the God who makes covenants. He is the Lord, the sovereign king. He is Jesus, the Savior. Each name He bears is a blessing He bestows on us.

Are you getting to know God? "And those who know Your name [who know God's nature] will put their trust in You" (v. 10). The better you know God, the more you will trust Him. The more you trust Him, the better you will get to know Him—an exciting and enriching experience.

♦ ♦ ♦

One of the great experiences of the Christian life is the personal relationship we enjoy with our God. To trust God is to seek Him (Isa. 55:6). Today, seek Him with a desire to know Him better.

IN HIS TIME

Have you ever looked at a beautiful rose and watched it slowly blossom day after day? Have you ever tried to help it open? If you try, you might kill it. God makes everything beautiful in His time. He causes everything to straighten out and line up according to His schedule. If you have a problem in your life with a person or a circumstance, rely on God to resolve it. "'Vengeance is Mine, I will repay,' says the Lord" (Rom. 12:19). One of the worst things we can do is to take judgment into our own hands.

The psalmist tells us in these verses, "Let God be the judge, the jury and the prosecuting attorney. He knows more about this than you do." The psalmist assures us that, in His time, God will catch those who are doing wrong. The nations will fall into the pit they have made. Sinners who have laid nets in the pathway will get caught in those nets. "The wicked is snared in the work of his own hands" (v. 16).

It encourages me to know that I don't have to devote my time or energy, even my inward concern, to wondering what's going to happen to all the evil in the world. God is going to take care of it. Of course, we as Christians should do our part to make this a better world. We are the salt of the earth; we are the light of the world. But we've been called to do something even more wonderful—to tell these wicked people that they don't have to go to hell. We have the privilege of witnessing to them and letting them know that they can be saved. Yes, let God be the Judge. Your job today is to be a witness.

♦   ♦   ♦

Has someone wronged you recently? Resist the urge to judge that person. Instead, pray that God might use you to reach the offender.

WHO'S RULING THE WORLD?

The humanist sings, "Glory to man in the highest." And some-times it looks as if man is prevailing and God is a failure. You recall the slogan that was popular a few years ago that pro-claimed "God is dead." Then the philosophers decided God was not really dead; He was simply sick and infirm and couldn't do much about what was going on in the world.

This mindset began in Genesis 3, when Satan said to Adam and Eve, "Look, why should you be a man? You can be like God." That's the same lie that runs the world today. Man is saying, "I will be like God."

But the psalmist tells us that man is not going to prevail. "The wicked shall be turned into hell, and all the nations that forget God" (v. 17). Today it looks as though man is succeeding—truth forever on the scaffold, wrong forever on the throne. But notice what David prayed: "Arise, O Lord, do not let man prevail, . . . that the nations may know themselves to be but men" (vv. 19,20).

If we take the scepter out of God's hand, we make a mess of things. God runs this universe, and He has ordained us to be under His au-thority. The word David used for man in verse 19 means "frail man, weak man." The problem today is that men don't know they are mere mortals; they think they're the Creator. And they worship and serve the creature rather than the Creator. But the sad thing is this: When men try to be God, they don't become God—they become animals. They sink lower than men and start acting like animals. That's why our world is in such a mess today.

I rejoice that I'm just a frail person. I need God. I can come to Him and say, "O Lord, give me the strength I need to glorify Your name today."

♦   ♦   ♦

We know that God is sovereign in His universe. His purposes will pre-vail. We may confidently submit to His authority and rest in His love, wis-dom and strength. Though we are frail, God is our strength. Let God be King of your life and glorify His name in all you do.

HOW NEAR IS GOD?

As we read the Book of Psalms, we find that David was constantly in and out of trouble. Some people say that Christians who really love the Lord will never be in difficult places. But that wasn't true of Moses; it wasn't true of David; and it certainly wasn't true of our Lord Jesus Christ! Our Lord ended up in the most difficult place of all—crucified on a Roman cross.

Listen to David: "Why do You stand afar off, O Lord? Why do You hide Yourself in times of trouble?" (v. 1). Here are those questions once again: "Why, Lord? Where are You?" Why do we think God is far away from us? What makes us think God has deserted us? First, we know that God is everywhere. Second, He has promised not to forsake us (Heb. 13:5). David only felt as if God were far away.

That's a good lesson for us to learn. Don't base your judgments only on your feelings. Build your life on faith. Faith says, "I'm going to trust God no matter what I see, no matter what I think and no matter how I feel." Faith does not mean we are ignorant. It means we are walking in the will of God because we know the Word of God.

Yes, David was in trouble. The proud and self-sufficient were after him. They were persecuting and taunting him, "I shall not be moved." They were also saying, "God won't see it" and "God will not judge." But David came to the Lord and said, "Lord, You know all about this, and You are going to take care of it."

When it seems as if God is far away, remind yourself that He is near. Nearness is not a matter of geography. God is everywhere. Nearness is likeness. The more we become like the Lord, the nearer He is to us.

♦   ♦   ♦

Do you desire to be nearer to God today? Fill your mind with the truth of the Word and your heart with prayer and trust God to take care of you.

THE HEART
OF THE PROBLEM

David cried out and said, "God, You've got to take care of the situation." For several years Saul had been pursuing him. At one point David compared himself to a flea that was being chased. Saul's problem was that he was listening to liars in his court. Those who wanted Saul's favor were saying, "David wants your crown. He wants your throne. David said this, and David did that." They lied about him, and he could do nothing about it.

We have little control over the circumstances of life. We can't control the weather or the economy, and we can't control what other people say about or do to us. There is only one area where we have control—we can rule the kingdom inside. The heart of every problem is the problem in the heart. Once we get to that throne room inside us and let God take over, we don't have to worry about others.

David prayed in verse 12, "Arise, O Lord! O God, lift up Your hand! Do not forget the humble." The word *humble* is a key word. What is humility? Is it thinking poorly of ourselves? No, humility is simply not thinking of ourselves at all. Humility means admitting that I cannot handle my problem by myself. God is going to have to handle it by working *in* me and *through* me and *for* me. But before God can work for me or through me He has to work in me.

If you want to get on top of your circumstances, get beneath the feet of the Lord. Humble yourself, and He'll lift you up.

♦ ♦ ♦

We cannot control the circumstances of life, nor can we avoid them. But we can take a humble attitude toward God. He takes a special interest in us and will help us handle our circumstances. Have you examined the throne room inside lately? Are you willing to let God work in you and through you to accomplish His purposes?

THE QUESTION "WHY?" PART 1

"**W**hy?" is the easiest question to ask but the hardest to answer. David asks why three times in this psalm. The atheist's answer to this question is that there is no God; the rationalist says God is unable to act or doesn't care; and the legalist says this is punishment for personal sin. The truthful answer comes from David. There are three stages in this experience of asking why.

The first stage is *concern—God is hiding.* People have asked for centuries, "Why doesn't God do something?" (Job 13:24; Jer. 14:8,9). The wicked seem to be triumphing, and in doing so, they make four false statements. First, they say, "There is no God" (vv. 1-4; Ps. 14:1). The fool worships the creature, not the Creator. The greatest judgment God can send is to let us have our way. He is the source of life. When we leave out God, we die. Do you consider Him when you make plans?

Then the wicked say, "I shall not be moved" (vv. 5-7). They curse the God they do not believe in. They enjoy the taste of sin. Third, the wicked say, "God does not see me." They picture Him as a ferocious beast, catching the innocent unawares. They are characterized by hypocrisy, deception, intimidation, threats and selfishness. This graphically pictures many into today's business world.

Finally, the wicked say that "God does not care." But He does care, and sin will catch up with them.

◆　　◆　　◆

Most of us at some time find ourselves asking God "Why?" Although the world offers several answers to this question, the Bible gives us insight into how to deal properly with the question. Don't be like the wicked, who make false statements about God and defy His judgment. Rest in the promises of the Word of God.

THE QUESTION "WHY?"
PART 2

I n Part 1 we dealt with *concern*—the first stage of asking the question "Why?" In this segment we will cover the last two stages.

The second stage involves *commitment—God is helping*. Man's sinful condition leaves him helpless, so David turns his attention from the wicked to God. We can be encouraged by knowing that God *sees* our trouble and *knows* our grief (v. 14). Objectively, He knows what we face; subjectively, He feels what we feel. Phillips Brooks said, "The purpose of life is the building of character through truth." Character is built in the storms and battles of life; it is tested in the easy times of life. The most discouraging feeling is that nobody understands. Christ endured all His earthly experiences so God could prepare Him to be a merciful and faithful High Priest. We may also be encouraged by knowing that God *investigates* (v. 15). He sees and cares, and He will repay (v. 14).

The third stage in asking "Why?" deals with *confidence. God is hearing* (vv. 16-18). "Man of the earth" is the wicked, living for and because of the earth. David reminds us that we're just mortal men (Ps. 9:20). God hears when we call and remembers; in His time, He accomplishes His purposes. And we can be confident of that.

A day of reckoning will come when the wicked will suffer for their unrepented sin. God has appointed His Son to be the judge. If you don't know Christ as Savior, if you think you're getting away with sin, or if you wonder why God doesn't do something, be thankful that He has not judged you yet (II Pet. 3:9). Jesus died for you and will save you if you will trust Him.

♦   ♦   ♦

God does not turn a deaf ear to our questions. Nor is He inactive regarding sin. He is interested in helping us build character, and He will accomplish His purposes in due time. If you're a Christian and wondering why God doesn't act, commit yourself to the Lord and place your confidence in Him (Ps. 37:5).

WANT TO RUN AWAY?

✦

Have you ever felt like running away? "In the Lord I put my trust; how can you say to my soul, 'Flee as a bird to your mountain'?" (v. 1). All of us have days when we feel like quitting. We throw up our hands and say, "That's it. I've had it, and I'm leaving."

At times we do need to get away to rest and regain our perspective. Our Lord Jesus said to His disciples, "Let's just depart and rest a while." Vance Havner once remarked, "If you don't come apart and rest, you'll just come apart." But the psalmist was not talking about a vacation. "The wicked bend their bow" (v. 2). He was saying, "The wicked are doing this and that. Let's get out of here and go to some mountaintop and have a good Bible conference."

When you feel like running or flying away, remember, God's throne is secure. The Lord is in His holy temple. In a difficult time Isaiah looked up and saw the Lord on His throne, high and lifted up. In the Book of Revelation, John saw the Lord on His throne, and it gave him new courage.

Don't flee to a mountain; flee to the throne of grace. When you feel like quitting or running away, remember that you can't run away from your troubles and you can't run away from yourself. The solution is not running *away*; it's running *to*. It's running to the throne of grace and finding grace to help in time of need.

✦ ✦ ✦

Those times when you feel like quitting can be times of great opportunity, for God uses your troubles to help you grow. When you feel like running away, claim your privilege as a child of God and approach the throne of grace. There you will find the personal and tailored help you need.

THE ELIJAH COMPLEX

Whenever you get the idea that you are the only one left who is godly, beware. That's how David was praying in Psalm 12. He said, "The godly man ceases! For the faithful disappear from among the sons of men" (v. 1). I call this the Elijah complex. You will remember that Elijah had this problem (I Kings 19). He left his place of ministry, went out into the wilderness and sat down, pouting. God asked, "What are you doing here?" Elijah replied, "I'm the only godly one left, and they are trying to kill me." God said, "I have 7000 people waiting in line. I can pick any one of them to get My work done."

When you begin to think you're the only godly person, it quickly leads to pride. In this passage David refers to the sin of flattery (v. 2). Our world is filled with flattery. Sometimes it's called advertising or promotion, but it's still flattery. God doesn't flatter people. He tells the truth. Flattery is manipulation, not communication. It comes from a double heart, from mixed motives. David said, "Unite my heart to fear Your name" (Ps. 86:11). Don't fall for flattery or flatter yourself into thinking you are the only godly one left.

Verse 6 tells us where to turn: "The words of the Lord are pure." Listening to your own words may lead to discouragement or pride. And the words of others may be flattery, lying or vanity. So listen to the Word of God and test everything you hear by it.

The godly person has not completely vanished from the earth. We'd be surprised to find where God has His people, waiting to accomplish His will. Others are waiting to stand with you and help you. Lay hold of God's Word. It has been tested and proved. You can trust it.

♦　　♦　　♦

The remedy for discouragement is the Word of God. When you feed your heart and mind with its truth, you regain your perspective and find renewed strength. Feeling discouraged? Encourage yourself with the Word of God.

PURE WORDS

When you feel deserted, alone in standing for what's right, read Psalm 12. The emphasis in this psalm is on words, on speaking. First, *David speaks in prayer* (vv. 1-3). Where are the godly? People today don't want to take a stand for the truth, but David stood for what is right.

Sometimes we feel the faithful have disappeared—those who believe in prayer, giving and commitment. Today's generation doesn't believe in commitment, especially with our words. We hear so much empty talk, lies and flattery. Flattery is manipulative, not communicative, like our advertising and some of our preaching.

Second, *the wicked speak in pride* (v. 4). Never underestimate the power of speech. Jesus told the truth; His enemies argued. He gave words of life; they rejected Him. He came in love; they crucified Him. One of the evidences that a person is giving the truth of God's Word is that he is rejected. People don't want to hear truth unless they belong to truth (John 10:4).

Third, *God speaks in promise* (vv. 5,7). His words are pure, not empty lying (v. 6). But the words of the wicked will burn in the furnace. God's Word is precious, because it cost Jesus' life. It is proved (v. 6) and permanent (v. 7). He keeps His promises. God knows where His people are, and He helps them. "I will arise"; "I will protect"; "I can be trusted" (vv. 5-7).

✦　　✦　　✦

So much that is spoken in this world is untrue and empty talk. Be encouraged that God speaks in promise. His Word is pure and true. When you are surrounded by lies, rest on the promises of the Bible.

HOW LONG CAN YOU WAIT?

Have you ever been impatient with God? Impatience is one of my big problems. I always get into the wrong lane on a toll road. Someone's in front of me with foreign currency, trying to buy his way through the tollbooth. I get into the wrong line at the airport, thinking, *This line is a good line; it's going to move.* But it doesn't because somebody in the line has lost his passport. And I get irritated.

It's one thing for us to be impatient with ourselves or with others. But when we become impatient with God, we should watch out! "How long, O Lord? Will You forget me forever? How long will You hide Your face from me? How long shall I take counsel in my soul?" (vv. 1,2). Four times David asked, "How long?" We're so time-conscious today. We have watches that show us split seconds. But what do we do with those split seconds? If we save three minutes by taking a shortcut, what significant thing will we accomplish with the three minutes we save?

We expect God to do what we want Him to do—and right now! But He doesn't always act immediately. Abraham had to wait for 25 years after God's promise before Isaac was born. Isaac had to wait 20 years for his children. Joseph had to wait 13 years before he was set free and put on the throne. Moses had a wait of 80 years. You see, God's schedule is not the same as ours. Sometimes He waits so that He can do more for us than we expect. When He heard that Lazarus was dying, our Lord waited until his friend's death before He came. But when He came, He brought a greater miracle and received greater glory. The hardest thing to do is to wait on the Lord. But we can if we will trust Him and rest on His Word.

♦   ♦   ♦

Some of your greatest blessings come with patience. When you must wait for God to act, you can be confident that He knows what is best for you and what will best glorify Him. Are you waiting for God to act on your behalf? Align with His timing and rest on the promises of His Word.

WHO'S A FOOL?

The word *fool* in Psalms or Proverbs does not refer to an unintelligent person. It refers to a person who is morally perverse. Why is he a fool? Because "the fool has said in his heart, 'There is no God'" (v. 1). And what is the result of this? "They are corrupt, they have done abominable works, there is none who does good" (v. 1). God looks down and says, "Does anybody have a clean heart?" The answer is no.

The fear of the Lord is the beginning of wisdom (Prov. 9:10). When people don't fear God, they have no wisdom, spiritually or otherwise. The fool says, "There is no God," which is practical atheism. Most of the world today lives by the philosophy that says, "There may be a God, but I'm not going to think about Him." God is not in their thoughts, and consequently, He is not in their lives.

The two words "there is" in verse 1 are in italics, which means they were added by the translators to help complete the meaning of the verse. We can read this: "The fool has said in his heart, 'No God.'" The fool not only says that there is no God; he also says *no* to God. When we say no to God, we are telling Him that we know more about life than He does and that we have more authority than He has. We cut off ourselves from the blessing He wants to give us.

Rejecting God involves a man's whole being. "The fool has said in his heart" (v. 1). There we have the heart. In verse 2 God looks down to see if any understand. That involves the mind. "They have all turned aside, . . . there is none who does good, no, not one" (v. 3). There we have the will. Verses 1-3 show the heart, mind and will possessed by sin, because somebody has said, "No God." If you want peace, say yes to God. All of His promises are yes in Jesus Christ (II Cor. 1:20).

✦ ✦ ✦

The most foolish thing you can do is leave God out of your life. If you do, you cut off your source of life and blessing. Don't make the mistake of the fool. Turn to the Lord and submit to His authority.

ARE YOU WORTHY?

Imagine what would happen if I walked up to the main gate at Buckingham Palace in London and said to one of the tall, handsome, well-dressed guards, "Sir, I want to live with the royal family." He would look at me and say, "Begone, before I arrest you."

Who is worthy to live with God? Only through Jesus Christ can we "dwell in God's holy hill." David always was a little bit envious of the priests. When we read the Psalms, we find David saying such things as, "Oh, those priests. They are able to walk in the temple of God. I can't do that. I can't go into the Holy Place." Spiritually he could, but physically he couldn't. Because we are in the Lord Jesus Christ, we can come boldly into the presence of God, not just to visit Him but to live with Him.

David describes the kind of person who is able to live with God. He must have the right kind of feet ("walks uprightly") and hands ("works righteousness"), lips ("speaks the truth") and heart. What we say with our lips always has to come from our heart. Verse 3 also talks about the tongue: "He who does not backbite with his tongue, nor does evil to his neighbor, nor does he take up a reproach against his friend." This is the person God welcomes at His front door and says, "You come and live with Me." That person has clean feet, clean hands and a clean heart that produce clean words and clean motives, one in whose eyes a vile person is despised. His eyes look upon only what is right and good.

Here is a beautiful picture of the kind of person God chooses to live with Him. And the beauty of it is this: Such a person will never get an eviction notice. "He who does these things shall never be moved" (v. 5). How can we be this kind of person? Through faith in the Lord Jesus Christ.

✦   ✦   ✦

God welcomes those with clean feet, clean hands and a clean heart. Remember, your worth is founded in Jesus Christ. It is through faith in Him that you are acceptable in the sight of God. Are your feet, hands and heart clean?

A DAY OF DELIGHTING

This is a psalm of delight. We find no trials or tribulations in this song. David is simply delighting, first of all, *in the Lord*. "You are my Lord, my goodness is nothing apart from You" (v. 2). In other words, he is saying, "I have no good beyond God."

Then David delights *in the Lord's people*. "And to the saints who are on the earth, 'They are the excellent ones, in whom is all my delight'" (v. 3). Do you delight in God's people? "To live above with saints we love will certainly be glory. To live below with saints we know, that's another story." Are some of God's people becoming abrasive to you? Start delighting in the Lord, and you'll start delighting in His people.

David also delights *in God's providence*. "You, O Lord, are the portion of my inheritance and my cup; you maintain my lot. The lines have fallen to me in pleasant places" (vv. 5,6). God, in His providence, knows where to draw the line. Problems arise when people don't know where His lines are. They want to keep moving the line. Let God give you your inheritance. When Israel went into the Promised Land, He gave each tribe its inheritance. It wasn't done by a real estate agent or by a lottery. God said, "Here are the lines. Maintain those lines." Do you want to delight in God and in His people? Then delight in His providence.

David also finds delight *in God's pleasures*. Verse 11 has been my life verse for many years. "You will show me the path of life; in Your presence is fullness of joy; at Your right hand are pleasures forevermore." Do you want life and joy? Here's the secret: Live on God's path, live in His presence and live for His pleasures.

✦ ✦ ✦

You have much to delight in—God's people, His providence and His pleasures. The key to delighting in the things of God is to delight in God Himself. Sometime today take a moment to simply delight in the Lord and praise Him for who He is.

HEAR ME,
HOLD ME, HIDE ME

Three words summarize David's cry in Psalm 17. The first word is *hear*. "Hear a just cause, O Lord, attend to my cry" (v. 1). David was saying, "I want the Lord to hear me, because my heart is right." "You have tested my heart" (v. 3). When did God do that? "You have visited me in the night" (v. 3). The dark times of life are when God proves us. He also proves Himself to us—if we let Him. When you're going through the darkness, when the night has come, when you can't see any light, remember, He is proving you and proving Himself to you. God knew that David's heart was right. "Hear a just cause, O Lord" (v. 1). Remember, when you're in the darkness, when you're in danger, when you're facing difficulties, God will hear you.

The second key word is *hold*. Uphold my steps in Your paths, that my footsteps may not slip" (v. 5). David wasn't simply standing still, doing nothing. He was on the move. When we're in the darkness, we move one step at a time as the Lord directs us. We don't just sit still and wonder what is going to happen next. David was saying, "God, I'm going to get moving. You've got to hold me up. Direct me; I don't want to slip and fall." Jude must have known this verse. He wrote, "Now to Him who is able to keep you from stumbling, and to present you faultless before the presence of His glory with exceeding joy" (Jude 1:24).

The third word is *hide*. "Keep me as the apple of Your eye; hide me under the shadow of Your wings" (Ps. 17:8). A shadow is not good protection. But if it's the shadow of God's wings, we can depend on it. What wings did David refer to? The wings of the cherubim in the Holy of Holies. David was saying, "I'm coming to the very throne of God. Please hide me and hold me and hear me." God replied, "David, I'll do it. I'm going to carry you through your dark time."

✦   ✦   ✦

Everyone must face dark times. God allows times of testing because He uses them to accomplish His purposes. Are you facing a difficulty today? Remember, God is faithful. He will hear you and direct you through the darkness. Let Him prove you, and give Him opportunity to prove Himself to you.

FIGHTING A
SPIRITUAL BATTLE

Prayer is essential to the Christian life. God commands us to pray (Luke 11:2; 18:1; I Thess. 5:17), and He uses people of prayer. What are the elements of an effective prayer life? First, *we need God's ear—"hear me."* David was praying for "a just cause"; he was concerned about God's will. But God won't hear us if we harbor deliberate sin in our lives, if we pray with "deceitful lips." He loves us too much to pamper us in our sins. To get God's ear, we must pray honestly, fervently and submissively. We must prepare our hearts for prayer.

Second, *we need God's eye—"examine me."* David could have killed Saul on two occasions, but by faith he left his vindication with the Lord. God knew David's heart. He probes our hearts when we pray. Often we are like Jacob; we pray and then meddle and scheme. We must not pray and then gossip. God's Word and prayer go together. If we live by the Word of God, it keeps us in the will of God.

Third, *we need God's hand—"deliver me."* The word *save* (vv. 7,13) means "deliver." Notice that David's response is one of submission, and God's response is one of service. King David asks the King of kings for help, and He responds to David's faith. His enemies think they have David, but God's power goes to work for him.

Finally, *we need God's face—"satisfy me."* If our praying doesn't make us more like our Lord, our praying is in vain (Josh. 24:15). God's goal is that we be conformed to the image of His Son (Rom. 8:29). But we don't have to wait for the resurrection; we can be changed daily through God's Word and through prayer.

The purpose of prayer is to accomplish the will of God, for us to become like Jesus.

♦   ♦   ♦

God uses your prayers to accomplish His will, both in your life and in the lives of others. To be effective, your prayers need God's help. Make your prayer time an alignment to His Word and His will.

A Song
of Deliverance

Psalm 18 celebrates David's victory over his enemies. Notice the inscription at the beginning. This is the song David sang "on the day that the Lord delivered him from the hand of all his enemies and from the hand of Saul." David did not classify Saul as one of his enemies. Isn't that interesting? David was an enemy to Saul, but Saul was not an enemy to him.

We may not be able to prevent other people from being our enemies, but we can prevent ourselves from being enemies toward others. Our job is not to create problems and make enemies. Our job is to pray, to live for the Lord and to represent Him in all we do.

The Lord delivered David from all his enemies. The Hebrew language contains 23 different words for *deliverance*. The Jewish people knew something about deliverance. Throughout their history God had delivered them.

Who delivered David? God did. When did He do it? When David called upon Him. "I will love You, O Lord, my strength" (v. 1). As we look at verses 1-6, we find nine different titles for God: my God, my Rock, my Fortress, my Deliverer, my Strength, my Shield, the Horn of my Salvation, my Stronghold, the Lord. Don't let that little word *my* upset you. You must lay hold of God personally and say, "He is my God. He is my Deliverer. He is my Salvation." Who delivers you? The Lord. When will He deliver you? When you call upon Him. "I will call upon the Lord, who is worthy to be praised; so shall I be saved from my enemies" (v. 3).

♦   ♦   ♦

David learned how to trust God for deliverance. Although his circumstances were often difficult, God was his Stronghold, and David called on Him for help. Do you need deliverance? Is God your Deliverer? If so, you may call on Him for help.